Customer Service Representatives;

Last-Minute Bottom Line Job Interview

Preparation Questions & Answers for any

Customer service professional Job

Why this Book:

This book tries to bring together the important information for a last minute preparation in as low as 60 minutes for a career in Customer Service. In this book you will find the most frequently asked job interview questions for both support center and call center environments. It covers questions related to excellent customer service, respecting the customer's time, customer development, workflows, processes and business needs, customer relations, problem resolution, time management, effective customer service, customers' expectations, customers inquiries, customer feedback, resolve problems.
It has been well written to make it a very quick read. It also covers non-technical,
HR and Personnel questions in brief.

This is useful for these job interviews:

Customer Service Representatives
Call Center Customer Service Representative
Customer service professionals
Customer Development Representative
Business Service Representative
Customer Account Representative

Copy Right

BLGSLLC

Pennsylvania, USA

All rights reserved. No part of this may be used or reproduced in any form or by any means, or stored in a database or retrieval system, or transmitted or distributed in any form by any means, electronic, mechanical photocopying, recording or otherwise, without the prior written permission of author or publisher. The information provided is for only instructional value. This book is sold as is, without warranty of any kind, either expresses or implied. This e-book is provided "as is" without warranty of any kind, either express or implied, including, but not limited to, the implied warranties of merchantability, fitness for a particular purpose, or non-infringement. In no event shall the authors or copyright holders, publisher, distributor be liable for any claim, damages or other liability, whether in an action of contract, tort or otherwise, arising from, out of or in connection with the book or the use or other dealings in the book.

This publication could include technical inaccuracies or typographical errors. Changes are periodically added to the information herein; these changes will be incorporated in new editions of the publication. While every precaution has been taken in the preparation of this book, the publisher and the author assume no responsibility for errors or omissions. Neither is any liability assumed for damages resulting from the use of the information or instructions contained herein. It is further stated that the publisher and author are not responsible for any damage or loss to your data or your equipment that results directly or indirectly from your use of this book. All products mentioned in this book are trademarks, registered trademarks or service marks of the companies referenced in this book. This note is not sponsored, endorsed or affiliated by any associated vender.

Trademarks: All trademarks are the property of their respective owners; BLGS LLC is not associated with any product or vendor mentioned in this book.

Index

Customer Service Representatives; Last-Minute Bottom Line Job Interview Preparation Questions & Answers for any Customer service professionals Job

Customer Service Representative Job Interview Questions?

As a Customer Service Representative define a Customer?

How you manage Time as a Customer Service Representative?

What Telephone skills you have to serve as Customer Service Representative?

As customer service representative how you maintain professionalism?

As Customer Service Representatives how will you handle a difficult customer?

As customer service representatives how will you measure productivity?

What kind of customer service representatives you are?

As customer service representatives define a Good customer service?

As customer service representatives what Customer Call Differentiating means to you?

As customer service representatives how you handle customers complains?

As customer service representatives how you define a customer and service?

As customer service representatives how you define excellent service?

As customer service representatives how you want to treat customers?

As customer service representatives what conflict resolution tools you have used?

As customer service representatives what soft skills you have?

As customer service representatives why you need Emotional Intelligence?

As customer service representatives how will you execute problem-solving outcome?

As customer service representatives what Communication channels have you used?

As customer service representatives how you resolve conflict?

As customer service representatives what strategies you follow?

As customer service representatives how you deliver negative news?

As customer service representatives how you resolve conflict?

As customer service representative how you discuss a problem?

As customer service representative what expectations customers have from you?

As customer service representatives why you need good personal hygiene?

As customer service representatives how you maintain a professional appearance?

As customer service representatives how you maintain personal hygiene & good grooming?

As customer service representatives good service important?

As customer service representatives how you handle rush hour service?

As customer service representatives list types of guests?

As customer service representatives what customer needs in reference to Maslow's Hierarchy?

As customer service representatives what categories of customers you have handled?

As customer service representatives list Customer Competency levels?

As customer service representatives what Characteristic makes you Excellent Leader?

As customer service representatives why you value Existing Customer?

As customer service representatives what barriers of Listening you encountered?

As customer service representatives what Methods of Communication you have used?

As customer service representatives what factors you think prevents excellent customer service?

As customer service representatives what are the motives you have observed?

As customer service representatives what Communication channels you have used?

As customer service representatives have you used Customer Relationship Management (CRM)?

What is the responsibility of customer service Manager?

As customer service representatives why you think customer service to employees is important?

As Customer Service Representatives what listening skills you have?

As Customer Service Representatives how you apply Active Listening?

As customer service representatives have you used non-verbal communication?

As Customer Service Representatives what Netiquette you follow for emails?

As Customer Service Representatives what kind of Job Stress you have handled?

As Customer Service Representatives how you manage emotional labor?

As Customer Service Representatives have you used E-service?

As Customer Service Representatives explain your experience with E-service?

What will you tell customer to Troubleshoot Internet connectivity and slowness?

In windows how will you verify if network adapter setup correctly?

Non Technical/Personal/HR interview: Complimentary

Bottom Line Job interview?

Interview Question?

What are your greatest strengths?

What are your greatest weaknesses?

Had you failed to do any work and regret?

Where do you see yourself five years from now?

How Will You Achieve Your Goals?

Why are you leaving Your Current position?

Why are you looking for a new job?

Why should I hire you?

Aren't you overqualified for this position?

Describe a Typical Work Week?

Are You Willing to Travel?

Describe the pace at which you work?

How Did You Handle Challenges?

How do you handle pressure? Stressful situations?

How Many Hours Do You Work?

Why are you the best person for the job?

What are you looking for in a position?

What do you know about our organization?

What are your short term goals?

What Salary are you looking for?

Tell me more about yourself.

Why did you leave your previous job?

What relevant experience do you have?

If your previous co-workers were here, what would they say about you?

Where else have you applied?

What motivates you to do a good job?

Are you good at working in a team?

Has anything ever irritated you about people you've worked with?

Is there anyone you just could not work with?

Tell me about any issues you've had with a previous boss.

Any questions?

Why did you choose this career?

What did you learn from your last job experience?

Why is there a gap in your resume?

How do you keep current and informed about your job and the industries that you have worked in?

Tell me about a time when you had to plan and coordinate a project from start to finish?

What kinds of people do you have difficulties working with?

What do you want to be in 5 years?

Ideal career?

Responsibilities?

Dream job?

Skills?

What sets you apart?

If the project not gone as planned?

If unable to meet Deadlines?

Interpersonal skill?

Improve?

What do you feel has been your greatest work-related accomplishment?

Have you ever had to discipline a problem employee? If so, how did you handle it?

Why do you want this position?

Why are you the best person for this job?

What about Technical writing?

How versatile you are? Can you do other works?

How do you manage time?

How do you handle Conflicts?

What kind of supervisory skills you have?

Any Bad Situation you could not solve?

Anything else?

End

About the author

Customer Service Representative Job Interview Questions?

Suggested Answers

As a Customer Service Representative define a Customer?

I. A customer is person who buys goods or a service
II. Anyone with whom we exchange value with is a customer

How you manage Time as a Customer Service Representative?

I. I follow a Time management strategy
II. I plan time by making timetables,
III. I make schedules and to-do lists,
IV. I Prioritize activities and
V. I eliminate unnecessary or unhelpful activities from schedules,
VI. I Avoid time wasters,
VII. I Target the most important tasks

What Telephone skills you have to serve as Customer Service Representative?

I. I answer professionally
II. I answer promptly and being prepared
III. I make sure the conversation is over
IV. I handle upset callers
V. I keeping conversations professional
VI. I smile over the phone
VII. I speak clearly & naturally
VIII. I thank people for calling
IX. I use courtesy titles

As customer service representative how you maintain professionalism?

I. I am patient
II. I have positive attitude
III. I am resourceful
IV. I am responsible
V. I am sincere
VI. I am tactful
VII. I am ethical
VIII. I have integrity
IX. I am flexible
X. I am adaptable
XI. I am loyal
XII. I am friendly
XIII. I am enthusiastic

As Customer Service Representatives how will you handle a difficult customer?

I. I will use 5 A's : 1 Acknowledge, 2 Assure, 3 Affirm, 4 Appreciate, 5 Apologize
II. I will let the customer speak
III. I will review the company policies
IV. I will reflect on feelings
V. I will clarify
VI. I will diffuse
VII. I will appreciate the customer

As customer service representatives how will you measure productivity?

I measure productivity by:

  I. Results of Customer Surveys
  II. Feedback Received
  III. Objectives Met
  IV. Referrals Gained
  V. Reviews Received
  VI. Targets Achieved

What kind of customer service representatives you are?

I. I am competent
II. I am dependable
III. I am responsive

As customer service representatives define a Good customer service?

I. Exceeding the customer's expectations
II. Treating customers with a friendly attitude

III. Solving problems
IV. Offering solution

As customer service representatives what Customer Call Differentiating means to you?

I. A customer's psychological needs must be met when resolving incidents
II. My customer service operations must satisfy customers' psychological needs

As customer service representatives how you handle customers complains?

I. I Seek the Best Solution
II. I try to reach Agreement
III. I Work on acceptable solution
IV. If not then I reach out to management

As customer service representatives how you define a customer and service?

I. Customer: Anyone with whom we exchange value with.
II. Customer Service: The treatment one gives a customer

As customer service representatives how you define excellent service?

I. The 5 A's Acknowledge, Assure, Affirm, Appreciate, Apologize
II. Good Service
III. Innovation
IV. Quality

As customer service representatives how you want to treat customers?

I. Respect
II. Kindness
III. Patience
IV. Consideration

As customer service representatives what conflict resolution tools you have used?

　I. **Effective Listening:** actively understand information provided by the customer
　II. **Empathy:** to understand and share the feelings of customer

As customer service representatives what soft skills you have?

The attitudes or personality traits that can contribute to a person's success, such as

   I. Courtesy
  II. Listening skills
 III. Problem solving,
 IV. Conflict resolution and
  V. Critical observation.

As customer service representatives why you need Emotional Intelligence?

Emotional intelligence (EI) is also called emotional quotient (EQ).
It's the capacity of individuals to recognize their own, and other people's emotions,
3 major components of Emotional Intelligence are:

I. Self-Awareness

II. Emotional Management of Self of Others

III. Emotional Connection

As customer service representatives how will you execute problem-solving outcome?

　　　I. Quick response
　　　II. Effective resolution
　　　III. Skillful discussion
　　　IV. Caring attitude
　　　V. Managed easily

As customer service representatives what Communication channels have you used?

   I. Email
  II. In person
 III. Telephone
  IV. Text messaging
   V. Voice mail

As customer service representatives how you resolve conflict?

I. Everyone has opportunity to voice opinion

II. Everyone remain calm

III. Everyone finding areas of agreement

IV. Everyone exploring a variety of solutions including compromise

V. Everyone reaching a firm decision that meets the needs of the team

As customer service representatives what strategies you follow?

I. Treat customers with respect, listen politely to their complaints and questions
II. Do something special - reduce fees, give discount, etc.
III. If you make a mistake admit it. Once everyone knows what happened - can take steps to fix it.

As customer service representatives how you deliver negative news?

I. Clearly explain the problem

II. Remain professional

III. Show that you understand how this creates a problem for the recipient and apologize

IV. Show you are handling the situation fairly

V. Indicate your interest in an ongoing business relationship

As customer service representatives how you resolve conflict?

I. Listen carefully
II. Offer a resolution
III. Accept blame
IV. Correct the mistake

As customer service representative how you discuss a problem?

I. I give an opportunity for those who disagree to present their ideas.

II. I allow all team members' viewpoints to be heard
III. I address concern for the people and the situation
IV. I try to reach a firm agreement that works for everyone
V. I always do what is best for the business

As customer service representative what expectations customers have from you?

I. Quick response time

II. Skillful performance

III. Positive personal treatment

As customer service representatives why you need good personal hygiene?

   I. It affects rapport with guests
   II. I help us to keep feeling good
   III. I am representing the Company

IV. For Safety
V. For Comfort
VI. To Build Confidence & Pride

As customer service representatives how you maintain a professional appearance?

I. Follow Dress Code & Keep Uniform Clean/Pressed
II. Maintain Good Posture
III. Do Not Chew Gum/Food
IV. Maintain Good Grooming Habit
V. Attend To Personal Hygiene In Private

As customer service representatives how you maintain personal hygiene & good grooming?

    I. Prevent body odor by deodorant
   II. Facial hair trimming
  III. Keep my nails clean and healthy
  IV. Keep my hair clean & controlled
   V. Keep my teeth clean & breath fresh
  VI. Keeps hands away from hair & face
 VII. Wash my hands often

As customer service representatives good service important?

    I. To Stay Open
    II. To Have Customers Return
    III. To Have Customers Invite Other Customers
    IV. To Make Money

As customer service representatives how you handle rush hour service?

    I. Advanced Preparation

II. Teamwork

III. Professional Attitude

As customer service representatives list types of guests?

I. Internal - co-workers & suppliers

II. External - customers that use products & service

As customer service representatives what customer needs in reference to Maslow's Hierarchy?

  I. Physiological Need :food, shelter, sleep
 II. Safety Need :safe consumption, not be robbed
III. Love & Belonging Need :acceptance by peers
IV. Esteem Need customers business is valued
 V. Self-Actualization Need confident & comfortable

As customer service representatives what categories of customers you have handled?

   I. Cater-to-Me
  II. SOCIALIZES
 III. Celebrator
  IV. Impulsive
   V. Busy-Bee

As customer service representatives list Customer Competency levels?

I. Unconscious Incompetence: One don't know that one don't know
II. Conscious Incompetence: One is now aware that one is incompetent at something
III. Conscious Competence: One develop a skill in that area but have to think about it
IV. Unconscious Competence: One is good at it and it now comes naturally

As customer service representatives what Characteristic makes you Excellent Leader?

I. I show care and respect for all
II. I practice what I preach
III. I behave professionally
IV. I give support to team
V. I practice consistency
VI. I demonstrate flexibility
VII. I have expertise in my field

As customer service representatives why you value Existing Customer?

I. They know how our products and services.
II. They buy without sale pitch

As customer service representatives what barriers of Listening you encountered?

I. Closed mind to the speaker and message.
II. Distraction.
III. The listener won't stop talking.
IV. Uncommitted listening.

As customer service representatives what Methods of Communication you have used?

    I. Listening
   II. Reading
  III. Talking
  IV. Writing

As customer service representatives what factors you think prevents excellent customer service?

I. Attitude
II. Stress
III. Laziness
IV. Moodiness
V. Communication
VI. Management

As customer service representatives what are the motives you have observed?

I. Rational Motive   Based On Logical Reason

II. Patronage Motive   Based On Loyalty

III. Emotional Motive   Based On Feelings

As customer service representatives what Communication channels you have used?

I. Email
II. In person
III. Telephone
IV. Text messaging
V. Voice mail

As customer service representatives have you used Customer Relationship Management (CRM)?

   I. Yes, I used information about customers to create marketing strategies for customer retention
   II. Used CRM to keep customers by building long-term relationships
   III. I used it to develop and sustain desirable customer relationships

What is the responsibility of customer service Manager?

I. To provide guidance to employees
II. To train employees to the challenge

As customer service representatives why you think customer service to employees is important?

I. Stimulates Initiative
II. Promotes Learning
III. Teaches Responsibility

As Customer Service Representatives what listening skills you have?

Listening is key to all effective communication, my approach:

　　I. Listening
　　II. Understanding
　　III. Responsive

As Customer Service Representatives how you apply Active Listening?

I. Understand
II. Interpret
III. Evaluate

As customer service representatives have you used non-verbal communication?

Interpersonal communications that are not expressed verbally are called non-verbal communications.

There are many different types of non-verbal communication I have used for Effective communication

As customer service representatives:

I. Body Movements
II. Posture
III. Eye Contact
IV. Facial Expressions

V. Physiological Changes

As Customer Service Representatives what Netiquette you follow for emails?

Netiquette is the Communication rules on the internet.

I make sure my emails cover these:

I. Subject lines: Correct keywords and phrases
II. Salutations: Thank you

III. Draft, cc, bcc
   IV. Body of email
   V. Closing

As Customer Service Representatives what kind of Job Stress you have handled?

   I. Career
   II. Workload
   III. Interpersonal
   IV. Management
   V. Roles

As Customer Service Representatives how you manage emotional labor?

In order to fulfill emotional requirements I have managed the feelings and expressions:

    I. Display Rules: Job Requirements
    II. Emotional Labor: Effort Exerted
    III. Emotional Performance: Observed Expressions

As Customer Service Representatives have you used E-service?

I. E-Service stands for electronic service

II. Uses information and communication technologies (ICTs) in different areas

III. For example E-Banking uses computer networks to make electronic funds transfers

IV. Some other examples are automated appointment confirmation Blogs etc.

As Customer Service Representatives explain your experience with E-service?

Advantages of E-service

    I. It saves time and money for companies

    II. It offers convenience for customers

Disadvantages of E-service

    I. It causes Misunderstandings

    II. There is no direct human interaction in the virtual e-service process

Non Technical/Personal/HR interview: Complimentary

Bottom Line Job interview?

Bottom-line: You will learn to answer any questions in such a way that you match your qualifications to the job requirements.

Interview Question?

Example response. Try to customize your answers to fit the requirements of the job you are interviewing for.

What are your greatest strengths?

I. Articulate.
II. Achiever.
III. Organized.
IV. Intelligence.
V. Honesty.
VI. Team Player.
VII. Perfectionist.
VIII. Willingness.
IX. Enthusiasm.
X. Motivation.
XI. Confident.
XII. Healthy.
XIII. Likeability.
XIV. Positive Attitude.
XV. Sense of Humor.
XVI. Good Communication Skills.
XVII. Dedication.
XVIII. Constructive Criticism.
XIX. Honesty.

XX. Very Consistent.
XXI. Determination.
XXII. Ability to Get Things Done.
XXIII. Analytical Abilities.
XXIV. Problem Solving Skills.
XXV. Flexibility.
XXVI. Active in the Professional Societies.
XXVII. Prioritize.
XXVIII. Gain Knowledge by Reading Journals.
XXIX. Attention to details.
XXX. Vendor management skills.
XXXI. Excellent Project Management skills.
XXXII. Self-disciplined.
XXXIII. Self-reliant.
XXXIV. Self-starter.
XXXV. Leadership.
XXXVI. Team-building.
XXXVII. Multitasking.
XXXVIII. Prioritization.
XXXIX. Time management.
XL. Can handle multiple projects and deadlines.
XLI. Thrives under pressure.

XLII. A great motivator.

XLIII. An amazing problem solver.

XLIV. Someone with extraordinary attention to detail.

XLV. Confident.

XLVI. Assertive.

XLVII. Persistent.

XLVIII. Reliable.

XLIX. Understand people.

L. Handle multiple priorities.

LI. Build rapport with strangers.

What are your greatest weaknesses?

I. I am working on My Management skills.
II. I feel I could do things on my own in a faster way without delegating it.
III. Currently I am learning to delegate work to staff members.
IV. I have a sense of urgency and I tend to push people to get work done.

V. I focus on details and think thru the process start to finish and sometimes miss out the overall picture, so I am improving my skills by laying a schedule to monitor overall progress.

Had you failed to do any work and regret?

I. I have No Regrets.
II. I am Moving on.

Where do you see yourself five years from now?

I. I am looking for a long-term commitment.
II. I see a great chance to perform and grow with the company.
III. I will continue to learn and take on additional responsibilities.
IV. If selected I will continue rise to any challenge, pursue all tasks to completion, and accomplish all goals in a timely manner.

V. I am sure if I will continue to do my work and achieve results more and more opportunities will open up for me.
VI. I will try to take the path of progression, and hope to progress upwards.
VII. In the long run I would like to move on from a technical position to a management position where I am able to smoothly manage, delegate and accomplish goals on time.
VIII. I want to Mentor and lead junior-to-mid level reporting analysts.
IX. I want to enhance my management experience in motivating and building strong teams.
X. I want to build and manage relationships at all levels in the organization.
XI. I want to get higher degree, new certification.

How Will You Achieve Your Goals?

Advancing skills by taking related classes, professional associations, participating in conferences, attending seminars, continuing my education.

Why are you leaving Your Current position?

   I. More money
   II. Opportunity
   III. Responsibility
   IV. Growth
   V. Downsizing and upcoming merger, so I made a good, upward career move before my department came under the axe of the new owners.

Why are you looking for a new job?

I have been promoted as far as I can go with my current employer.

I'm looking for a new challenge that will give me the opportunity to use my skills to help me grow with the company.

Why should I hire you?

    I. I know this business from ground up.
    II. I have Strong background in this Skill.
    III. Proven, solid experience and track record.
    IV. Highest level of commitment.
    V. Continuous education on current technical issues.
    VI. Direct experience in leading.
    VII. Hands-on experience.
    VIII. Excellent Project Management skills.
    IX. Demonstrated achievements.
    X. Knowledge base.
    XI. Communications skills.
    XII. Ability to analyze, diagnoses, suggests, and implements process changes.
    XIII. Strong customer service orientation.

XIV. Detail oriented, strong analytical, organizational, and problem solving skill.
XV. Ability to interact with all levels.
XVI. Strong interpersonal, relationship management skills.
XVII. Ability to work effectively with all levels, cultures, functions.
XVIII. I am a good team player.
XIX. Extensive Technical experience.
XX. Understanding of Business.
XXI. Result and customer-oriented.
XXII. Strong communication skills.
XXIII. Good Project and Resource management skills.
XXIV. Exceptional interpersonal and customer service skills.
XXV. Strong analytical, evaluative, problem-solving abilities.
XXVI. Good management and planning skills.
XXVII. Good Time Management skills.
XXVIII. Ability to work independently.
XXIX. I've been very carefully looking for the jobs.
XXX. I can bring XX years of experience.

XXXI. That, along with my flexibility and organizational skills, makes me a perfect match for this position.

XXXII. I see some challenges ahead of me here, and that's what I thrive on.

XXXIII. I have all the qualifications that you need, and you have an opportunity that I want. It's a 100% Fit.

Aren' t you overqualified for this position?

I. In My opinion in the current economy and the volatile job market overqualified is a relative term.

II. My experience and qualifications make me do the job right.

III. I am interested in a long term relationship with my employer.

IV. As you can see my skills match perfectly.

V. Please see my longevity with previous employers.

VI. I am the perfect candidate for the position.

VII. What else can I do to convince you that I am the best candidate? There will be positive benefits due to this. Since I have strong experience in this ABC skill I will start to contribute quickly. I have all the training and experience needed to do this job. There's just no substitute for hands on experience.

Describe a Typical Work Week?

I. Meeting every morning to evaluate current issues.
II. Check emails, voice messages.
III. Project team meeting.
IV. Prioritize issues.
V. Design, configure, implement, maintain, and support. Perform architectural design. Review and analysis of business reports.
VI. Conduct weekly staff meetings.
VII. Support of strategic business initiatives.
VIII. Any duties as assigned. Implementation.
IX. Monitor and analyze reports. Routine maintenance and upgrades.
X. Technical support.
XI. Deploy and maintain.
XII. Provide day-to-day support as required. Work with customers and clients.

XIII. Documentation.
XIV. Standard operating procedures.
XV. Tactical planning.
XVI. Determine and recommend.
XVII. Plan and coordinate the evaluation.
XVIII. Effective implementation of technology solutions.
XIX. To meet the business objectives.
XX. Participatation in budget matters.
XXI. Readings to Keep Abreast Of Current Trends and Developments in the Field.

Are You Willing to Travel?

I. For the right opportunity I am open to travel.
II. I'm open to opportunities so if it involves relocation I would consider it.

Describe the pace at which you work?

I. I work at a consistent and steady pace.
II. I try to complete work in advance of the deadline.

III. I am able to manage multiple projects simultaneously.
IV. I am flexible with my work speed and try to conclude my projects on time.
V. So far I have achieved all my targets
VI. I meet or exceeded my goals.

How Did You Handle Challenges?

I. Whenever the project got out of track I Managed to get the project schedules back on the track.
II. Whenever there was an issue I had researched the issues and found the solutions.
III. We were able to successfully troubleshoot the issues and solve the problems, within a very short period of time.

How do you handle pressure? Stressful situations?

I. In personal life I manage stress by going to a health club.
II. I remain calm in crisis.
III. I can work calmly with many supervisors at the same time.
IV. I use the work stress and pressure in a constructive manner.
V. I use pressure to stay focused, motivated and productive.
VI. I like working in a challenging environment.
VII. By Prioritizing.
VIII. Use time management
IX. Use problem-solving
X. Use decision-making skills to reduce stress.
XI. Making a "to-do" list.
XII. Site stress-reducing techniques such as stretching and taking a break.
XIII. Asked for assistance when overwhelmed.

How Many Hours Do You Work?

I enjoy solving problems and work as much as necessary to get the job done.

The Norm is 40 hour week.

Why are you the best person for the job?

　I. It's a perfect fit as you need someone like me who can produce results that you need, and my background and experience are proof.
　II. As you can see in My resume I've held a lot of similar positions like this one, and hence I am a perfect fit as all those experiences will help me here.
　III. I believe this is a good place to work and it will help me excel.

What are you looking for in a position?

　I. I'm looking for an opportunity where I may be able to apply my skills and significantly contribute to the growth of the company while helping create some advancement and more opportunities for myself.

II. It seems this organization will appreciate my contributions and reward my efforts appropriately to keep me motivated.

III. I am looking for job satisfaction and the total compensation package to meet My Worth that will allow me to make enough money to support my lifestyle.

What do you know about our organization?

I. This is an exciting place to work and it fits my career goals.

II. This company has an impressive growth.

III. I think it would be rewarding to be a part of such a company.

What are your short term goals?

I'd like to find a position that is a good fit and where I can contribute and satisfy my professional desires.

What Salary are you looking for?

   I. Please provide me the information about the job and the responsibilities involved before we can begin to discuss salary.
   II. Please give me an idea of the range you may have budgeted for this position.
   III. It seems my skills meet your highest standards so I would expect a salary at the highest end of your budget.
   IV. I believe someone with my experience should get between A and B.
   V. Currently I am interested in talking more about what the position can offer my career.
   VI. I am flexible but, I'd like to learn more about the position and your staffing needs.
   VII. I am very interested in finding the right opportunity and will be open to any fair offer you may have.

Tell me more about yourself.

I. I'm an experienced professional with extensive knowledge.
II. Information tools and techniques.
III. My Education.
IV. A prominent career change.
V. Personal and professional values.
VI. Personal data.
VII. Hobbies.
VIII. Interests.
IX. Describe each position.
X. Overall growth.
XI. Career destination.

Why did you leave your previous job?

I. Relocation.
II. Ambition for growth.

III. This new opportunity is a better fit for my skills and/or career ambitions.
IV. To advance my career and get a position that allows me to grow.
V. I was in an unfortunate situation of having been downsized.
VI. I'm looking for a change of direction.
VII. I want to visit different part of the country I'm looking to relocate.
VIII. I am looking to move up the with more scope for progression.

What relevant experience do you have?

I have these XYZ related experience.

I have these skills that can apply to internal management positions et al.

If your previous co-workers were here, what would they say about you?

Hard worker, most reliable, creative problem-solver, Flexible, Helping

Where else have you applied?

I am seriously looking and keeping my options open.

What motivates you to do a good job?

Recognition for a job well done.

Are you good at working in a team?

Yes.

Has anything ever irritated you about people you've worked with?

I've always got on just fine with all my co-workers.

Is there anyone you just could not work with?

No.

Tell me about any issues you've had with a previous boss.

I never had any issues with my boss.

Any questions?

Please explain the benefits and bonus.

How soon could I start, if I were offered the job?

Why did you choose this career?

    I. Life style.
    II. Passion.
    III. Desire.
    IV. Interesting.
    V. Challenging.
    VI. Pays Well.
    VII. Demand.

What did you learn from your last job experience?

I gained experience that's directly related to this job.

Why is there a gap in your resume?

Because of Personal and family reasons I was unable to work for some time.

Unemployed.

Job hunt.

Layoffs.

How do you keep current and informed about your job and the industries that you have worked in?

   I. I pride myself on my ability to stay on top of what is happening in the industry.
   II. I do a lot of reading.
   III. I belong to a couple of professional organizations.
   IV. I have a strong network with colleagues.
   V. I take classes and seminars.
   VI. I have started and participated in many technical blogs.

Tell me about a time when you had to plan and coordinate a project from start to finish?

   I. I headed up a project which involved customer service personnel and technicians.

II. I organized a meeting and got everyone together.
III. I drew up a plan, using all best of the ideas.
IV. I organized teams.
V. We had a deadline to meet, so I did periodic checks with various teams involved.
VI. After four weeks, we were exceeding expectations.
VII. We were able to begin implementation of the plan.
VIII. It was a great team effort, and a big success.
IX. I was commended by management for my managing capacity.

What kinds of people do you have difficulties working with?

I. I have worked in very diverse teams.
II. Diversity means differences and similarities with men and women from very diverse backgrounds and culture. It helps us grow as a human being.
III. The only difficulty was related to work related dishonesty by a person.
IV. He was taking credit for all the work our team accomplished.

What do you want to be in 5 years?

I hope to develop my management skills by managing a small staff.

Ideal career?

    I. I would like to stay in a field of ABC.
    II. I have been good at ABC.
III. I look forward to ABC.

Responsibilities?

I would expect expanded responsibilities that could make use of my other skills.

Dream job?

Includes all of the responsibilities and duties you are trying to fill.

I also thrive in the fast changing environment where there is business growth.

Skills?

I was very pleased to develop the A, B, C skills that you are seeking

What sets you apart?

I. Once I am committed to a job or project I take it with tremendous intensity.
II. I want to learn everything I can.
III. I am very competitive and like to excel at everything I do.

If the project not gone as planned?

Backup and identify precautions.

If unable to meet Deadlines?

    I. Negotiate.
    II. Discussion.
    III. Restructure.
    IV. Redefine Optimum goal.
    V. Show a price structure.

Interpersonal skill?

    I. I had to learn to say no.
    II. Helpful to other staff.
    III. Help in return.

Improve?

In any job I hold I can usually find inefficiencies in a process, come up with a solution.

What do you feel has been your greatest work-related accomplishment?

I. Implemented an idea to reduce expenses, raised revenues.
II. Solved real problems.
III. Enhanced department's reputation.

Have you ever had to discipline a problem employee? If so, how did you handle it?

Problem-solving skills, listening skills, and coaching skills.

Why do you want this position?

    I. I always wanted the opportunity to work with a company that leads the industry in innovative products.
    II. My qualifications and goals complement the company's mission, vision and values.
    III. I will be able to apply and expand on the knowledge and experience, and will be able to increase my contributions and value to the company through new responsibilities.

Why are you the best person for this job?

    I. I have extensive experience in XYZ (Skill they are looking for)
    II. I'm a fast learner.

III. I adapt quickly to change.
IV. I will hit the ground running.
V. I'm dedicated and enthusiastic.
VI. I'm an outstanding performer.
VII. I may be lacking in this specific experience but I'm a fast learner and I'll work harder.

What about Technical writing?

I. I can convert any complex technical information into simple, easy form.
II. I can write reports to achieve maximum results.

How versatile you are? Can you do other works?

I am flexible and can adapt to any changing situations.

How do you manage time?

I. I am very process oriented and I use a systematic approach to achieve more in very less time.
II. I effectively eliminate much paperwork.

How do you handle Conflicts?

I. I am very tactful;
II. I avoid arguments and frictions and
III. I establish trust and mutual understanding.

What kind of supervisory skills you have?

I. I make sure that everyone understands their responsibilities.
II. I try to be realistic in setting the expectations and try to balance the work among all.

Any Bad Situation you could not solve?

I've never yet come across any situation that couldn't be resolved by a determined, constructive effort.

Anything else?

   I. I am excited and enthusiastic about this opportunity
   II. I am looking forward to working with you.

End

About the author/editor/compiler: BLGS team enjoys sharing their expertise on wide variety of subjects in easy language to help all readers.

Copy Right: Just-in-time E-books/BLGS Publishers

BLGS LLC USA

BLANK PAGE

Disclaimer of Warranty, No Liability:
THE INFORMATION, CONTENTS, GRAPHICS, DOCUMENTS AND OTHER ELEMENTS INCLUDED HEREIN (COLLECTIVELY THE "CONTENTS") ARE PROVIDED ON AN "AS IS" BASIS WITH ALL FAULTS AND WITHOUT ANY WARRANTY OF ANY KIND.
Restrictions on use of content per Internet Privacy act.
The content is copyright © BLGS. BLGS is independent training provider. All rights reserved. You cannot reproduce by any methods such as linking, framing, loading positing to blogs et al, transfer, distribute, rent, share or storage of part or all of the content in any form without the prior written consent of BLGS .its solely for your own non-commercial use. You may not change or delete any proprietary notices from materials received. We assume no responsibility for the way you use the content provided. All these notes files on this site are here for backups for personal use only. If you are sharing any information from here with any third-party you are violating this agreement and Internet Privacy act.

General Jurisdictional Issues:
Terms of Use will be governed by the laws of the Bucks County in the state of Pennsylvania in USA without respect to its conflict of laws provision

DMCA:

All materials here are created with the good faith. All the references if any to copyrighted or trademarked materials are only for references and discussions. These notes do not replace any related vendors documentations. Readers are encouraged to buy and refer to the related vendors documentations and books. These notes are intended for personal use only. The use of any acronym or term on or within any BLGS product, content, website or other documentation should not be considered as impinging on the validity, ownership, or as a challenge to any trademark, logo or service mark. All other trademarks are the property of their respective owners, and the aforementioned entities neither endorse nor sponsor BLGS or its products. These notes or any material produced by this company is not sponsored by, endorsed by or affiliated with SUN,HP, IBM, and Microsoft, Cisco, Oracle, Novell, SAP,RED HAT,VERITAS,LEGATO,EMC,NETAPPS or any other company. All trademarks are trademarks of their respective owners. All these interview notes Content are not sponsored by, endorsed by or affiliated with any other company. Any Copyright, Confidential Information, Intellectual Property, NDA, or Trademark or Service mark infringements discovered on or within notes and the products and services will be immediately removed upon notification and verification of such activities.
Please send your feedback to: bottomline@interview-guru.info

www.ingramcontent.com/pod-product-compliance
Lightning Source LLC
Chambersburg PA
CBHW060401190526
45169CB00002B/699